One Glorious Night

James R. Fogg Jr.

WESTBOW
PRESS®
A DIVISION OF THOMAS NELSON
& ZONDERVAN

WestBow Press books may be ordered through booksellers or by contacting:

WestBow Press
A Division of Thomas Nelson & Zondervan
1663 Liberty Drive
Bloomington, IN 47403
www.westbowpress.com
1 (866) 928-1240

ISBN: 978-1-9736-1602-3 (sc)
ISBN: 978-1-9736-1601-6 (e)

Library of Congress Control Number: 2018900716

Print information available on the last page.

WestBow Press rev. date: 01/19/2018

Dedication

I WISH TO DEDICATE THIS book primarily to my descendants, from children and grandchildren down to great- and great-great-grandchildren yet unborn. May my story inspire them, just as I am inspired by my ancestors, such as John Longest (my grandma Fogg's grandfather), killed in the Civil War. Bloodlines and past experiences influence our lives more than we realize. Another hope for this work is that all who read it will be moved and transformed to live more purposeful and devoted lives.

Preface

I, Jᴉᴍ Fᴏɢɢ, ᴡʜɪʟᴇ ʜᴜɴᴛɪɴɢ elk in Routt National Forest, Colorado, in October 2016, lived through a life-changing experience. I promise never to forget it.

I am a seventy-eight-year-old Sunday school teacher who is neither senile nor crazy. I clearly saw my surroundings and fully realized my experiences on that most memorable night and early morning of October 18 through October 19. Very plainly, my Lord is with me now and forever.

Acknowledgments

I WOULD BE REMISS IF I did not give credit to and say thanks to an inspirational Christian lady in Winters, Texas, whom I have never met. She is Leigh Powers, a pastor's wife, freelance writer, and graduate of Baylor University. This fine lady wrote the series of Sunday school lessons from which I taught on Sunday, October 30, 2016. This book's section titled "The Heavenly Vision" was extracted from her series of lessons, which were so very enlightening.

Also, I am thankful for my King James Bible, from which I quote Matthew 18:11–13 in this book to clarify my take on my experience.

Introduction

WHO AMONG US CAN PEER into the future to discern what lies ahead as we work and play in our everyday lives? Only our Creator knows. Most of our days terminate with varying degrees of success; some days strike us as gleefully satisfying as we lay our heads on our pillows at night. Sadly, sometimes fate can unexpectedly turn against us to test our will and fortitude. When that happens, we simply must, in order to survive, use every available tool in our arsenals to rejoin our dear families and friends. Such was the predicament that this author found himself in during a thirty-hour stretch from October 18 to October 19, 2016. Only his fine physical shape for seventy-eight years of life, his undying determination, and especially his strong faith in our Lord and fervent prayer pulled him through.

One Glorious Night

(October 18–19, 2016)

WHAT IS ONE GLORIOUS NIGHT for a man who has lived for over seventy-eight years? Surely there have been many memorable days and nights throughout such a long span, but all others pale in comparison to the night beginning at six thirty in the evening on October 18, 2016, and lasting until ten o'clock in the morning on October 19, 2016. I survived that night in a mountainous region of Routt National Forest in the snow and brutal cold by divine intervention.

In order to explain this night, I must jump back to late March 1968—forty-eight and a half years ago. In my younger days, I was very hawkish about why we must halt the spread of Communism in this world, so I decided to volunteer for Vietnam to help slow down its advance. After

I returned from one year in Vietnam (March 14, 1967–March 14, 1968) as a US Air Force pilot, my wife, Mary Lou, and I were moving into on-base housing at McGuire Air Force Base, New Jersey. After having become reacquainted with each other on an eight-day leave (vacation) on the island of Jamaica, this was my new assignment.

When we moved in at McGuire, little did I realize I was about to strike up a lifelong friendship. There, living only fifty yards away, was another air force pilot whom I would soon join in the same squadron. His name was Bill Berringer, and his wife was Judy. They had two small children, a daughter named Robyn and her younger brother, Todd. Another son, Brett, would come along later.

After seeing me enter our new residence, Bill went into their home to tell Judy, "That man and I will become very good friends."

Judy said, "How do you know? You've never even met the guy."

Bill explained, "When I saw him enter their new home with three large armfuls of guns, I knew it."

Bill quickly came over to introduce himself. A deep friendship soon developed that would endure until he died in April 2013. I continue to live so far, but I miss his friendship. My wife, Mary Lou, and his wife, Judy, are like sisters. Bill was my brother.

Bill and I would very soon discover that we both had a

strong urge to hunt game. Hunting turkeys and pheasants was very good sport, but elk hunting would soon become our fever.

Soon after our meeting, Bill told me that he was planning to leave the air force to pursue a career as a commercial pilot. His choice was Western Airlines. I inquired, "Who is Western Airlines?" Bill explained that Western Airlines was to people out West what Eastern Airlines was to us folks back East. My plan all along had also been to join an airline to finish my flying career.

Bill joined Western Airlines in December 1968 and moved to Los Angeles. I followed him in May 1969 to Western Airlines and moved to Orange County, California. In the spring of 1972, my wife and I moved from Orange County to North Glenn, Colorado, which is north of Denver; we moved there with our three-year-old son, Randy, and our six-month-old daughter, Robyn. We named her Robyn because of our admiration for Bill and Judy's daughter of the same name and because it started with "R," as our son's name (Randy) did. Their names signified for us "R and R," which in the military stands for "rest and relaxation"—a Vietnam throwback.

Bill eventually moved to Niwot, Colorado, and we decided to go elk hunting above Colorado's Rabbit Ears Pass in 1972. We were joined by Bill's father, brother, brother-in-law, and two more of his relatives. Out of all seven of us, I had the good fortune to get our only bull elk: I pulled him from a herd of forty-four cows and calves. He was a giant—the only bull in the herd.

In June 1973, Bill and I went scouting to decide where to hunt elk in the fall. We parked our pickup at the Sheriff Reservoir trailhead and walked for miles into Routt National Forest, a wilderness area. For you flatlanders, a "wilderness area" is an area that prohibits *all* motorized vehicles. Absolute quiet is the order of the day. After crossing Bunker Creek and then coming down the west slope of Main Ridge of Bunker Basin, we ran into a large herd of elk. We decided to place our camp near the north tip of Spur Ridge, between Main Ridge and Quake Ridge, which is located four miles back into the timber from the nearest road.

Bill and I backpacked to the same spot that following October, set up camp, and hunted that season. Our families have hunted from that same camp every year since then, eventually extending the tradition to close friends. Ever since starting our camp we have hunted in a style that most hunters would not want to endure. Our hunting success through the years has been a direct result, we have felt, of the extra effort we have expended. Elk hunting season is too short to waste time "Holiday Inn" fashion. Our opinion has always been that leisurely getting up in daylight and having a nice hot breakfast in one's pickup camper is for sissies, not real dedicated elk hunters. Our hunting day always begins at five in the morning, when we crawl from our sleeping bags, get dressed in full hunting gear, grab our rifles, and quietly wish our companions a safe and successful hunt. We then each climb from our camp at 9,400 feet to our predetermined elk stand. We hunt up to an altitude of 11,300 feet. We eat nothing before leaving camp, as our food and water will have been packed in our backpacks and canteens since the previous night.

We always enjoy a great time together in our tent when evening comes. We relate the excitement of the day, tease one another, tell jokes, and map out our strategy and location for the following day's hunt while partaking of the gourmet hot food, such as beef stroganoff or spaghetti, that has been prepared by our loving wives before the bull elk rifle season, which always starts around the middle of October. Our tent has been there every hunting season since then, and it will continue to be there. (However, as I will be seventy-nine in 2017, I may have to hang it up. Climbing those ten-to-eleven-thousand-foot mountains on foot in deep snow is not as easy as it used to be when Bill and I were in our thirties. Our sons and grandchildren will eventually have to carry on this tradition without us.)

Hunting elk, for Bill, was very trying during our October hunt of 2012. Lymphatic cancer had taken a severe toll on his body. During that hunt I discovered Bill being helped by his oldest son, Todd, as Bill struggled to journey back to camp after a severe snowstorm. I joined them in getting Bill through the deep snow. He kept saying, "Just leave me here," each time he would fall into the snow. Todd and I kept saying, "Sorry, we must make camp." Do you wonder why Todd and I didn't just put one of Bill's arms over each of our shoulders and return to camp that way? Cancer had eaten a large hole under Bill's right arm, making it very painful for him and tough for us to transport him.

The next day, we had horses brought in to take Bill from elk camp to safety below. In early April of 2013, Bill called me to say that his time with us was nearing an end. He said, "Jim, you and Mary Lou come out to join me and my extended family for our last rendezvous." We did, and we had quality time that we cherished. We, along with our wives, watched our favorite of all movies, *Jeremiah Johnson*, before going out to a fine restaurant to dinner. The fact that Bill was able to endure so much activity at this late stage of his life speaks to the determination and stamina that he had been blessed with since birth. A week later we returned for Bill's funeral, where I delivered one of his eulogies.

Since then, Bill's two sons, Todd and Brett (later joined by his grandchildren, Matt, Brayden, Triston, and Kalyssa), and I have carried on the annual elk hunt. My son, Randy, hunted with me once when he was fourteen and decided that was enough torture for him to last a lifetime. I tried to explain that he had just experienced the coldest season we had ever endured but to no avail. He and his sons, along with his wife, Chrissie, now enjoy frequent snowboarding runs down Colorado's many ski slopes. Randy and my son-in-law, Kevin, are both airline captains. Todd and Brett are both United Airlines pilots. Poss Horton, who was my very close friend from Virginia Tech and my air force pilot training days, also hunted with us. He was a United Airlines captain and the chief pilot at Dulles Airport for many years. We lost Poss in April 2014, when I gave another eulogy. Brett also is a lieutenant colonel in the Colorado Air Guard, where he flies an F-16 fighter jet.

Bill and I both retired as Delta Airlines captains after being forced from flying at the age of sixty. I, being three years older than Bill, retired in 1998; Bill followed in 2001. Now pilots can fly to the age of sixty-five.

Because of our ties to flying, our camp has always been called That Airline Camp to those in the know, but very few know where it is. It is hard to locate, and it is well hidden by the forest until one is within thirty yards of it. Those of us who know That Airline Camp well have always been vague when sharing its location, elk hunters being the way they are. Many know of our successes. We have taken 111 bulls from the timber since 1972.

Enough of this reminiscing! Let's spring forward to the elk hunt of 2016, which transpired one month ago as I write this.

Our elk camp consisted of a total of seven. Bill's oldest grandson, Matt, who is one of Bill's daughter Robyn's twins, was there for the five-day season, October 15 to October 19. Bill's youngest son, Brett, along with his fourteen-year-old son, Brayden, who was a gleeful shooter of a big bull last year, was also there for the season. This five-day stretch was actually the short season, since it was the first rifle season. Bill's oldest son, Todd, along with his very pleasant thirteen-year-old daughter, Kalyssa, were there for the first three days. She was a real trouper, who sure enjoyed hunting with her dad. Todd left camp with Kalyssa on October 18 to get her back to school. Todd's son, Triston, hunted with us on opening day, but his season was cut short since he is a freshman—a "doolie"—at the US Air Force Academy. I was also there with the intention of hunting the entire season, or as long as the weather would allow.

Little did I know the dangers that lay ahead as I awoke to hunt at five in the morning, along with the rest of our camp, on Tuesday, October 18. October 15 to 17 had been pleasant hunting days except for the very strong, shifting winds that alerted the elk to our presence. Naturally, they were no-shows. Other than one bull moose and one spike bull elk, we saw none. Those two must have known we couldn't legally shoot them; it's illegal to shoot a moose during elk season, and a legal bull elk must have at least four points on one side. A spike bull is only one year old and has only one point per side.

In the dark of early morning on Tuesday, October 18, I climbed Quake Ridge near to the summit—an altitude above 10,500 feet. As daylight came, I gleefully noticed the many elk tracks around my stand. I had finally located the herd. *What a fine hunting day this is going to be*, I thought. Wrong! Little did I know the perils that awaited me.

The day started all right, as the wind finally stopped blowing and the sun shone bright. At around two thirty in the afternoon, the weather began to change as clouds rolled in. First came a downpour of sleet pellets, followed soon thereafter by snow that would obscure the sun for the rest of that day and the next morning. Still, I sat on my elk stand at the top of the mountain because with bad weather, the elk start to roam. They must eat before snow covers their food. However, that day none came into sight.

I had chosen that stand the afternoon before since we'd had good luck at the top of that ridge before. We always choose our stand according to the elk herd movements, which change almost daily. We discuss our stand locations the night before, since we don't want anyone else infringing upon our chosen location. We hunt alone after leaving camp each early morning.

On this particular October day, I finished my food around three thirty in the afternoon and drank my water canteen dry. *No problem, since I will have lots of water and food by seven o'clock tonight in camp*, I thought.

At six thirty that evening, with dark upon me and lots of snow, I departed my stand for camp. Camp was to the east across the lower beaver pond meadow and across the mountain. Not only was our camp obscured from other hunters, it could be hard to find at night even for us, especially in bad weather.

Upon reaching the small stream that flows fifty yards west of our tent, I knew that I had not approached the correct place to cross. I was either above or below camp, but which? In that blinding snow in the dark, a flashlight would have been nice. I checked my left coat pocket, where I always kept it, but to no avail. *I must have placed it by my stand at the top of the mountain and left it*, I thought. Too late; I was not going back for it then. I would have to find camp in the dark. Believing to be well above camp, I headed downhill just west of the stream. By then it had gotten pitch dark. The moon would be hidden by continuous snow clouds for the rest of that night.

Since I could not see my watch, I guessed it was around eight o'clock at night, so I fired my .30-06 rifle to alert my camp that I was lost. It was actually ten of eight, as I was informed the next day. The guys at camp quickly fired back. Suddenly I realized that I was well below camp. Whenever anyone was lost at night, the firing of our rifles was the procedure for rescue. In the past forty-three years, I had never been lost, but that night was different: I was seventy-eight years old and alone in a blinding snowstorm. The going had been very tough, as I'd had to climb over or under downed trees or walk way around them. The steep hills were especially tough as I neared mountain streams. Much snow and darkness greatly added to the problem. Also, I confess that I had never prayed so fervently in my entire life. I have believed strongly in my Lord my whole life and have prayed often. But when one believes that this could be one's last night, the person prays for help like never before. This was my case on that frigid night of October 18, 2016.

As the night wore on, I firmly believe I fell close to one hundred times, often sliding ten to twenty feet before catching my grip to stop my slide. If I fell and broke any bone, the situation would have become hopeless. After my first shot to notify the camp of my problem, my gun jammed on ejecting the round, so my rifle was useless from that point on. The rifle shell had jammed on extraction and would not let me clear the chamber for another round to be inserted. I love that rifle. It has brought down twenty-four bull elk for me, but my many tumbles into the snow had blocked its smooth workings.

My camp believed the worst for me, as my jammed gun meant I could not answer their rifle shots. Much later I would learn that Brett Berringer would venture out to assist me, but he also became lost in the night. His gun was not jammed, so his fourteen-year-old son, Brayden, and twenty-five-year-old nephew, Matt, would finally guide him back to camp. I heard those shots, but they were so far away they did me no good. I was not about to traverse those mountainous miles again; I just wanted to survive and come out to safety, if that were possible. Brayden and Matt told Brett that I could be dead, since I was not answering their gunshots. Brett replied, "Jim Fogg will make it somehow if anyone can." However, he was greatly worried.

My biggest mistake that night was crossing that stream onto Main Ridge in hopes of finding an easier walk up toward camp. I dreaded the thought of reversing my trek through all of that downed timber again and decided that climbing up the west slope of Main Ridge would be easier. There is a well-worn trail up that side that the elk and I have used, though not at the same time, for years. That night I guessed it would lead me back to camp in thirty minutes.

After the arduous task of traversing the stream, I

searched for that trail. Unfortunately, I crossed below where I suspected, so I found myself surrounded by heavy timber, both standing and fallen. Walking soon became quite difficult as I continued to try to discover a means to journey back to camp. Traveling uphill became nearly impossible. Realizing my dire situation, I decided to forget about reaching camp that night and to attempt to survive some other way. We have always said in camp that if you ever get lost, you should go downhill and walk out to civilization. Sounds easy enough, but just try it.

What you would think is the main ridge is actually one of the many ridges that lead off Main Ridge into Bunker Creek, which made our little creek by camp seem like a trickle in comparison. Traveling very slowly, slipping, and falling on steep ridges almost into the creek at times became perilous. As the night progressed, I lost my right mitten, which was filled with down, from my coat pocket. I wasn't using it anyhow, as I held onto my gun with my right bare hand while traveling and used it to catch myself as I fell over downed tree trunks and limbs. Neither my hands nor my body got cold, thanks to my constant traveling and racing heart! I did not realize it at the time, but my interior clothes were all wet from perspiration. My hunting coat had done a marvelous job of shedding the loose powder snow, so I was not wet on the outside, only on the inside! During the night on one of my tumbling-downhill falls,

I lost my prescription glasses. Searching for them proved fruitless, as my vision was impaired without them and my hands became numb from combing for them in the deep snow. I chose to waste no more time and proceeded without them.

I had a compass but could not see it in the darkness. I had a watch but had no idea what time it was all night since I had no light. Was it ten o'clock? Eleven? Twelve? One? Two? Three? Four? Five? The night seemed to endure for days. *Just survive, only survive*, I kept thinking, and I told myself to keep going downhill if that were possible. After one of my countless falls, a small voice seemed to whisper in my ear, "You have given it your best effort. You are completely given out. Just sit down on this log and rest. The end will come soon, and you won't hurt anymore!"

Then a louder voice from within seemed to say, "I refuse to give up. I shall use every ounce of my energy, never giving up, to find safety somehow. I must survive!"

My loving and sweet wife of over fifty-three years counts on me. We are inseparable. We have two dear children with remarkable spouses, four outstanding grandsons, and a precious granddaughter. I simply had to find a way to return to them all, but how?

Many hours later, with the night still dark, I stumbled from the downed timber into more open ground where sage and other brush grew.

What a relief, I thought. *I just may survive after all.* Finally free of the downed timber, my walking would become much easier, and I would fall much less often without the constant tree limbs hidden in the snow!

Farther downhill I encountered an unknown-to-me narrow road. *Where did this road come from?* I thought to myself. *I have not known of any road across the end of Main Ridge. Just the same, I'll try it.* Turning left on this road would lead uphill. I wanted to go downhill, so I turned right.

After walking about one hundred yards, I stumbled into a brand new problem. Charging at me, furiously snarling and barking, were two dogs apparently bent on gnawing both of my legs off. Each was at a thirty-degree angle to my left and right. With my heart in my throat, no gun for protection, and no possibility of outrunning them, I attempted to calm them down. What else could a fearful and very tired hunter do? I reverted to an old trick learned long ago: I kept saying, "Here doggie, doggie." It sounds silly, but in desperation I'll try anything. It worked! They halted and held me at bay.

Then, though extremely thankful for another hurdle overcome, I was left wondering, *What are these dogs doing here in the middle of the wilderness in a dreadful snowstorm?* A pack of wolves would maybe make sense, but not dogs. The mystery was soon solved when many hundreds of sheep began running past me from right to left at about twenty yards in front of me. The dogs were sheep dogs. As the last of the sheep sped past, both dogs left me, thank the Lord, and quickly followed the sheep. I then began to suspect where I had ventured. I was probably on Cross Mountain Ranch, a noted sheep ranch. I also knew my rescue would have to come from the adjoining Sombrero Ranch. I have known since 1973 that Cross Mountain Ranch borders Sombrero Ranch to the north. Our pickup was in fact parked at Sombrero Ranch, which is where we left to walk in to our camp. Both ranches contain thousands of acres, but their personnel do not get along at all: sheep and cattle ranchers do not mix. Do you remember the range wars of days long gone by? Well, the bitterness is still there.

Just the same, I needed to tread onward in the darkness. When I came to a fork in the narrow road, I decided to take the right one. After walking for about fifty minutes, I returned to the same fork, realizing that it was the start of a complete circle road of a very large sheep meadow. The only other way to travel this road would be uphill, which didn't make sense. I wanted to go downhill. Still, I took a few steps in that direction, strongly considering leaving that road altogether and traversing a new course straight down the point of the mountain to an eventual valley below.

I suddenly encountered an experience I shall never forget. Here, dear readers, is where the supernatural comes in! A bright light began to shine from my rear, lighting the road up ahead. It pointed up the road, just as if someone behind me were shining a strong flashlight past me, with my body blocking the center of the beam. I glanced to my left, right, and overhead; all around was darkness. What exactly was happening? Whenever I turned around, which was many times, all I saw was darkness. At times, I would start walking uphill and then suddenly snap my head rearward to catch my benefactor. My attempts were never fast enough. My source could never be tricked. How dare I try to compete with my higher power! Call me crazy if you'd like. I know 100 percent what I experienced.

After a long climb uphill, the road leveled and then turned downward; it remained lit up. It guided me then downhill—good news—into a valley, where I discovered a large home. I walked quickly to its front door and knocked, yelling loudly, "Please help me. I'm near exhaustion and desperate from walking all night in this snowstorm." No answer came from within. What time was it? Two o'clock in the morning? Three o'clock? Four? Five? I had no idea. I wondered, *Will they shoot me for invading their privacy?* Disappointed, I left that home to visit another home close by. I repeated my pleading actions and was met with the same result. Both were very nice homes, but what were they doing there with no one seeming about them?

After walking further downhill, I discovered six barns or sheds. One shed just beside the road had an open front into which you could drive a car. It was empty except for buckets and some mysterious piece of ranch equipment that I couldn't identify. It was too dark for me to figure out its purpose. At least the shed was dry inside, with a dirt floor, and I was out of the snow and wind finally! I leaned my rifle up by the entrance and searched for a place to sit. Finding a large bucket by the door I turned it upside down and sat, deciding to give my legs some needed rest.

Then, only a minute or two later, I began to shake all over from the cold. I was soaking wet from neck to toe from sweating during this very long night—a night that was not over yet. To prevent hypothermia from overtaking me, I was compelled to exercise every two or three minutes. By walking in place, stomping my feet, and moving both arms and shoulders in rapid succession, I was able to stop the shakes temporarily. Two points were certain: I did not want to allow the freezing weather to overtake me, which meant I absolutely must stay awake!

By the way, that light that guided me over that hill and down to that first home had disappeared. It did not return. What was it? You tell me. I know for sure it guided me, and I will always know for as long as I live, I promise!

Continually exercising in the shed to stop the shakes and stay awake, I felt my mouth was very dry. What I wouldn't have given for a quart of water to drink. Throughout that seemingly endless night I had been grabbing handfuls of snow with my left hand. My right hand had been busy with my gun, often using it as a prop with its stock into the snow. Mountain snow is not like our eastern snow; it is very dry. It was all I had though, so I bent often to get what I could of it into my mouth with my left hand. What time was it? I still didn't know. Would daylight ever come? What I knew was that my mouth was very dry, so I went back out front of the shed to grab more snow to put in my mouth. I peered up into the sky to witness something that will remain very clearly in my memory for the rest of my life. I promise that I shall never forget it. Never!

Overhead in the dark and continuously cloudy sky was a clear, bright figure with a head, a neck, and shoulders, but it had no visible torso or legs. From the shoulders down, the figure wore a long, flowing robe. I could not distinguish any eyes, nose, or other features—just a clear, round head. This figure was not ten thousand feet up in the sky; it had to be only one or two hundred feet over my head, since it was so dark and snowing so hard. For me, this form was unmistakable. It was Jesus Christ himself. Looking about those dark, low, obscuring clouds, I tried to envision any other possibility than my Savior's form, since

I knew this would be the most memorable experience of my life. I knew I would never want to have any reason to doubt or question it.

Therefore, I began roving my eyes about the entire snowy sky to learn if there were any other visible forms. I then saw another figure over to my right, by itself. It was sort of oval shaped and about one-fifth the size of the Christ figure. It appeared to have wings partially tucked by its sides. Both wings looked identical. Remembering my Bible, I concluded that this figure was the angel Gabriel.

Days later, I was told that Bill Berringer's son-in-law, Justin, told his family that he was convinced that this angel was Bill Berringer, sent from God and Christ to help his old buddy Jim from the timber to safety. "After all," Justin had said, "Bill and Jim came together into this great forest. Jim helped Bill back to camp during his last hunt of October 2012 in a severe snowstorm. Bill's body was wracked with pain from his cancer at the time. This time, October 2016, Jim was now the one in dire straits during a severe snowstorm, so why wouldn't Bill help his old dear friend out?"

Could Bill have been that angel? Why not?

I knew Bill very well. He was a *true* Christian. He did not curse, loved his Lord, and loved his family. I do not profess to be anything like an angel, but I have always endeavored to treat my fellow human beings with respect.

I truly love my Lord. My family and close friends mean everything to me. Like Bill, I have tried sincerely to be honest, fair, and just in all my transactions. Bill loved his wife, Judy, extremely. My devoted love is for my wife, Mary Lou. Mary Lou and I care very much for Judy, who still lives next door to her son, Brett, and Brett's family. Every one of those Berringers, without exception, is an outstanding person who loves the Lord.

So was that angel in fact Bill? I now believe it more than possible, though I cannot confirm it or the meaning of what I witnessed. I am just an earthling and must wait until the afterlife for clear understanding. We are not privileged to know such workings of our Lord.

What I do know *for sure* is what I clearly saw in that darkened sky no more than two hundred feet over my head. Those figures did not appear momentarily and then vanish; they remained unchanged and over my head for one or two hours. They were bright and clear figures in the dark sky. So that I would never think it possible that I may have been mistaken, I held on to the shed entrance for stability and continually stared at both figures to discern if there were any movement whatsoever. They both remained unchanged as I stared at them for about twenty minutes at a time, particularly the Christ one. I had been intensely praying all night long for help from my God and Lord Jesus, and finally I was talking out loud to Jesus directly. I was thanking him for guiding me down the mountain, saying, "I know that figure I see, Lord, is you. Please continue to help me find safety somehow. I am positive that you can and will guide me out." The only voice I heard all night was my voice pleading and thanking Jesus—well, my voice and the voices of those two pesky dogs bent on protecting their sheep.

After a long while of exercising, eating snow, and talking to my Lord, I noticed a slight easing of daylight rise into the eastern sky. "Hallelujah! This extremely long night appears to be over!" I exclaimed.

In a few minutes, daylight allowed me to see my watch. It was twelve minutes past seven o'clock. I could then see another barn and another home down below in the valley. I quickly made up my mind: *I'm going to go to that home, knock on the door, and yell for help. If there's no answer, I'll break a window and enter for water and protection from the elements. They can arrest me for breaking and entering. I don't care! I want to live!*

When I walked up on the front porch, I saw a sign on the door that read, "Please take your muddy boots off before entering this house." After shouting for help and hearing no answer, I decided to try the door before breaking a window. Much to my surprise, the knob turned and the door opened. I looked inside at a fully furnished home, but there was no sign of its owner. I closed the door. My snowy boots had no mud on them, but I still obliged: I sat on a bench just to the right of the door to remove my boots, both layers of my wet socks, and my hunting coat before I entered the home. No folks were there except me, thank goodness. I tried a light switch—no electricity. That was not a problem. The daylight amply lit the home. Water was what I most desperately needed, so I entered the kitchen and turned the faucet handle. No water was to be had. Then I went into the bathroom and tried for water; again there was none. There was water in the commode. *Good news! I shall drink it*, I thought. But when I bent down and cupped my hands for water, I saw a major problem. Floating in the water were many flies. No matter how thirsty I was, I had to pass on that liquid. The flies meant that no one had been in the home since warm weather.

Later I would learn that those three Cross Mountain Ranch homes are owned by "rich Californians." They only come there in the summer, apparently, pretending to be ranchers. The rest of the year the ranch, along with hundreds if not thousands of sheep and two fierce dogs is cared for by several sheepherders (they're not called *shepherds* out west) who had been in their own warm homes at the foot of the mountain with their families on that miserable night. Those dedicated and protective dogs would give up their lives before letting harm come to their beloved sheep. I certainly had no craving for a cutlet that night!

Still, I needed help. If I didn't have water, any liquid would do. Nope, there was no liquid—not even a Coke or 7 Up—to be had. The refrigerator and freezer were both bare, with doors wide open. Liquid seemed so near and yet so far away.

As I walked from the kitchen to the dining room, I noticed a telephone on the hutch at the far side of the table. I wanted to call for help, but I figured if there were no electricity there wouldn't be any phone service. Nevertheless, I tried the phone. Picking up the receiver, I heard a precious tone. Quickly, I dialed 911. An emergency operator named James answered. We soon became buddies. I told James who I was, my home address and phone number in Georgia, and my predicament. He was quickly alarmed by my trembling voice and said, "Shouldn't I send a rescue helicopter up there to get you?"

I said, "No, but I need someone to come from Sombrero Ranch to rescue me. Please notify the following people to tell them I am safe and alive," I said, and then I listed their names.

I did not want him to report that I was alive and *well*. *Alive*, yes, praise the Lord; but with blood oozing down both legs and both arms and hands scarred badly, I didn't think the word *well* was a proper description. I was elated to be safe and alive, and I wanted to relay the good news rapidly. My fear was that the word was out by then that Jim Fogg was history and had been lost for keeps in the storm. The thought that someone may have relayed this bad news to Mary Lou, who was with Judy Berringer in her home in Frederick, Colorado, gave me much alarm.

I told James over the phone to please call the state police and sheriff's department to say, "Jim Fogg, the lost elk hunter, is safe and alive!" James notified them immediately and told me they would *try* to come for me.

I said, "They can't come here. The snow is too deep, and besides, how can you tell where I am?"

James said, "The moment you picked up the phone and called me, I could pinpoint your location."

I said, "James, but there are three homes up here."

He said, "I know which of the three you are in." Wow, what modern technology!

Next I told James to call Brett Berringer's wife, Heidi. Brett was up in our elk camp, worried about me. I told James to have Heidi call Brett on his cell phone to say, "Jim is safe and alive." Then I wanted him to call Judy and Mary Lou to tell them the same good news. I wanted to eliminate any possibility of my wife receiving news of my probable demise. She would not have taken that well!

I also asked my newfound friend, James, to call Sombrero Ranch and tell Kevin, the ranch foreman, "Jim made it down the mountain" and that I hoped he could come and get me. James called me back to say he had notified Kevin and that he was coming for me.

I said, "I'm concerned that Kevin will not be able to drive up in the deep snow."

James said, "Don't worry. Kevin can make it in his four-wheel-drive high-center truck." Kevin arrived in front of the home at ten o'clock that morning, and what a beautiful sight. He quickly walked up on the porch, grabbing my coat and wet socks before I could exit the home. As I walked out on the front porch, Kevin said, "Put on your boots, Jim, so we can go." I didn't complain; I complied.

I couldn't thank Kevin enough! We returned to the shed to retrieve my trusty rifle. Normally I would have left it in the woods to rot away, since it was very tiring to drag along through the snow. However, I had often used it as a prop to help keep me from falling. I also knew what a valuable weapon it had been and would be again if I could only survive. It could be fixed. Plus, I had given it to my oldest grandson, Curt Fogg. He had loaned it back to me for hunting. You know how that goes! We can never hurt our grandchildren or anything that belongs to them.

As I alluded to earlier, James had informed me at the start of our conversation that my voice sounded shaky.

I had told him it was because I was still freezing and trembling. James said, "Can you find any type of coat to wear to warm up?" Looking in the living room, near the front door, I found a hunting coat I had not seen before and put it on. Almost immediately, I started to warm up, which James could tell from our following conversation. James was a jewel. I thanked him immensely before we hung up.

Also, on the dining room wall of that house had been a whiteboard and marker for writing notes. I took the marker and wrote on the board: "Jim Fogg, an elk hunter from Georgia, under dire circumstances, has entered your home to survive, but I have stolen nothing. I did borrow your hunting coat to keep warm, but I have returned it to your hanger. Thanks so much for the use of it and for your home."

While traveling back to Sombrero Ranch, I said to Kevin, "Do you have any water?"

"No," he answered, "but I'll soon give you all the water you can drink back at the ranch house."

I said, "Thanks. Lots of water, but please, no kind of alcoholic beverage."

When I informed Kevin of my prior night's hardships, he said, "Jim, I don't believe there is hardly any twenty-five-year-old man who could have survived those mountains last night in those conditions. It is even harder to believe you made it out at the age of seventy-eight years."

I said, "Kevin, I made it because I was not traveling alone."

He glanced at me with a look of confusion. He thought I had been alone up there. I said, "Kevin, I had wonderful help," as I pointed my index finger up toward the sky. He understood and smiled broadly. I related to Kevin all that went on that prior night.

Kevin was hardly a stranger. I had known him and his wife, Mary, from previous years of hunting there, and I also had known their fourteen-year-old daughter, Callie, who can handle a horse like a rodeo cowboy. Remember, Bill and I had hunted there since 1973, and I have continued every year since his death. Kevin is much younger than either of us, having only been the ranch foreman for about eight years. He is one fantastic person, as are his wife and daughter.

Upon reaching the ranch house, Kevin said, "Mary, fix Jim some breakfast. Jim, would you like to take a shower?"

"You bet! I would love to take a *hot* shower and clean off," I answered. "Mary, hold that breakfast a few minutes."

Kevin got me a pair of tennis shoes that fit me, clean socks, and a complete set of warm, dry clothes. Boy, what a treat! Kevin showed me the bathroom and said I could use *his* toothbrush over on the sink. I thanked him and said that I would—and I did. He was pleased. You see, out in cowboy land, we don't get nervous about hygiene issues. We do what is necessary and practical.

After my shower and getting dressed, I felt like a new man. Mary's breakfast for me, which I ate at eleven o'clock that morning, consisted of eggs over easy, strips of hog and elk bacon (I think, if that is possible), potatoes, a plate of pancakes with lots of syrup, and hot coffee. We ate high on the hog—or elk or beef—for the remainder of my stay. I stayed at the ranch house with them for the rest of that day and until the afternoon of the next, when Todd Berringer came to pick me up for our return to the plains north of Denver—Frederick, Colorado.

We were not alone at the ranch house the night I stayed. There must have been twelve to fifteen of us staying there, eating, and sleeping. Most were ranch hands, but three of us were hunters. Mary offered me a sleeping bag to place on one of the many bunk beds in the bunkroom for the night and said, "Will this be okay, Jim?"

I said, "Are you kidding? This if far superior to any of my bedding during this past week."

Knowing that Todd would soon come pick me up that day—Thursday, October 20—I went to Mary and said, "Mary, please tell me the charge for all your and Kevin's hospitality. There is no maximum charge, but I have a minimum fee that you must charge."

She said, "Jim, I don't handle finances. You have to talk to Kevin."

Later I cornered Kevin and gave him the same spiel. He said, "Jim, I am so happy that you survived. The bill will be nothing."

I said, "Kevin, you came over to that sheep ranch and got me, brought me here to safety, and treated me like a king for a day and a half. I feel compelled to pay you plenty."

Kevin said, "Merry Christmas, Jim. This is my present to you. I'm very happy to have helped you out of your problem. How you made it I will never know."

No amount of persuasion could change Kevin's mind. It wasn't as if he had received nothing for our hunt. We paid him to pack our tent, stove, food, etc. into camp at the start of the hunt and would pay him again to pack us out. That fee was not overcharging; it was fair. Kevin and Mary are gracious and honest people.

Todd came to get me later that Thursday afternoon to leave the mountains for our humble and loving wives on the plains. His brother, Brett, would walk out the four miles just as we all had walked in. Kevin's horses would transport all our hunting gear out.

When Todd said, "Are you ready to go?" I said, "Do you still have that one hundred dollars I gave you at the start of the hunt?" He said yes. I asked him for it so I could give it to Mary. She was outside, up on a few bales of hay atop the bed of a truck that was about to leave with horses to pack another camp out. I walked over and climbed up on one of the bales of hay in front of Mary.

"Mary," I said, "I tried to pay you, and you referred me to Kevin. I tried to pay Kevin, and he said, 'Merry Christmas.' I cannot think of enough words to thank you and Kevin for your help and generosity. What I can say is 'Merry Christmas to both of you and to your daughter, Callie.'" I slapped the one hundred dollar bill down onto the bale of hay in front of her.

Mary quickly grabbed the bill and attempted to hand it back to me, saying, "I'm sorry, Jim, I can't take this."

I backed away smartly and said, "Mary, you don't have any choice. I must leave now. Merry Christmas. Take that money, and treat yourselves to a very merry meal with food and drink of your and Kevin's choice."

I jumped into the truck with Todd, and we sped away.

I shall never forget them and will visit them again in the future. They are a family of three jewels. This world needs more people like them! We were too active to discuss politics during my whole stay, which is not a subject for busy people. That topic is reserved for folks with idle time on their hands, such as high school and college students and inner-city know-it-alls. We rural dummies are busy trying to make a living so we can send our children to college. Please forgive me for adding a bit of country humor here!

On the return trip I brought Todd up to speed on my experiences of the past two days. We arrived back at his mom's home, where Judy and Mary Lou awaited, around half past four that afternoon. They both had been alerted about my ordeal from James's phone message. Mary Lou was waiting for me in the yard on our arrival. She ran to me, crying, apparently glad to see me. Hugs and kisses abounded! I do believe that woman was pleased to see me again. After fifty-three years of marriage, we are more in love than ever!

At eight o'clock on that same night of October 20, Brett and his son, Brayden, arrived next door to where Judy, Mary Lou, and I were awaiting. They were returning from their hunt and bringing the camp gear home. They quickly came over to see me and compare notes on the past two days. As I discussed what I had experienced, we three cried like wee babes. The whole scene was just too emotional to handle after such a short span of time.

It is weird how we look at situations differently as time passes. What I perceived as confusion, torture, and pain on that long night, I now feel as almost a blessing sent from God and our Savior! Do we sometimes need our senses stressed immensely to shock us back into what really matters in life? As we race about each day while working, playing, sporting, and the like, do we take time to give thanks for our often undeserved yet bountiful blessings? Must we be reminded that we only have so much control? We have no control over the weather and little over fate.

Now that a month has passed, what is my take on my escape from death? The following is what I have concluded.

After going to church all my life and studying my Bible all that while, I only have a vague idea of where God is. It doesn't matter. We are not meant to know while pacing this planet. We just need to know that he loves us and wishes all good things for us. Whether we cause our own destruction or lose our earthly lives through no fault of our own, it matters little in the eternal course of events. God will always be in control.

Still, where is God? Where do I picture him? He must be up there, billions of miles away, on his glorious throne, overseeing all his creation; he can't just be on our small sphere known as earth. We are not allowed and do not deserve to picture God's home; it is everywhere.

So then, where is Jesus? I, like most of us, formed a picture long ago of him sitting at the right hand of God. If Christ is up there, can he still be here to look after you and me in our daily lives? Is he nearby? Why don't we see him, hear him, or get modern proof of his closeness? I lived for seventy-eight years on belief in Christ without proof; I did not feel I deserved any. I'm willing to venture a guess that you haven't any proof either.

Is it possible for Jesus to come down into view? If Christ were to appear to any single human being, wouldn't it be to the likes of Billy Graham or someone else far more deserving than I? Why me, Lord? I have always been a sinner, a bad sinner. I am the most sinful person I know. I know of all my sins and continually ask forgiveness for them, often repeating them. I know of almost no sin that you folks have committed. Most of you appear pretty clean and holy to me. I see you in church and about the community looking quite splendid. You don't look like sinners to me! Several of my friends have informed me that many people of faith commonly experience this feeling of guilt.

Maybe the biblical book of Matthew will help explain. I quote here from Matthew 18:11–13 verbatim from my old Holy Bible, King James Version, though I also own three more modern versions. I like this one best to describe my point. Hearken to the words of Jesus: "For the Son of man has come to save that which was lost. How think ye? If a man have one hundred sheep, and one of them be gone astray, doth he not leave the ninety and nine, and goeth into the mountains, and seeketh that which is gone astray? And if so be that he find it, verily I say unto you, he rejoiceth more of that sheep, then of the ninety and nine which went not astray."

Explain this to me, please! Was I a lost sheep in the mountains—maybe lost in more ways than one? Did my shepherd, Jesus, come into the mountains and rescue me? Just maybe the other "ninety and nine" of you did not need rescue. Think whatever you like. I am now contented. My heart is chock-full of gratitude for my Savior! Now I can face the winter of my life without fear. What I witnessed fills me with hope and confidence. Amen!

On returning to my home in Newnan, Georgia, I opened my Sunday school book (please see acknowledgments) to study the lesson that I would teach on the following Sunday at Central Baptist Church, where I have been active for these past twenty-eight years that we have lived here. I was shocked! The lesson heading was, "The Heavenly Vision." Its scripture was taken from Revelation 1:9–20. The section of descriptive reading starts with this statement: "Most of us have an image that comes to mind when we think of Jesus."

Near the conclusion of my lesson, I referred back to this statement and asked my class what their image of Jesus was. They answered what you would expect. They cited predictable images, such as, "A newborn babe in the Bethlehem manger," "Jesus walking on the sea," "Jesus healing the sick and disabled," and "Jesus overturning the tables of the money changers in the Temple." But mostly, of course, they pictured Jesus on the Cross of Calvary, atoning for our sins.

When they were finished, I stated my opinion. I said, "Not me. I have always had that same picture as you. Now I have a new image. Our Bible depicts Jesus walking our earth two thousand years ago. The Jesus that I know is the one who appeared to me two weeks ago in the Colorado Rockies." I then told them of my near-death experience. My firm statement was, "I used to believe; now I know for sure."

So once again, where is Jesus? He exists not just a million miles away up in heaven on the right hand of God but also hovering just over our heads, almost always out of sight. He loves us and watches us constantly. I praise God and Jesus for my rescue and for his appearance. I shall take that image to my grave with thankfulness. *Amen!*

God bless,
Jim Fogg (James R. Fogg, Jr.)

Epilogue

WHEN I CRAWLED FROM MY sleeping bag at five o'clock in the morning of October 18, 2016, I could not conceive of the extent to which I would be tested for the next thirty hours. I was excitedly hopeful that early October morning that fate would steer a big bull elk my way to end in success as had happened many times before. That would not be the case. Later, during that extended night, I kept thinking, *Why is this happening to me? Will I ever return from this dreadful situation alive?* In retrospect, I think of this elk hunt as my favorite of them all. I wouldn't trade my meeting with my Savior for all the elk in those hills. I feel so very fortunate to have experienced my Lord's appearance and help. For the first time in my life, I feel closeness with my surrounding Savior. It has transformed my thinking to a calming assurance that death, someday for me as also for you, will be only a transition, a stepping stone to a brighter future. Our Lord is with us all now and forever. Praise be to our God and Savior.

Author's Note

I HAVE SOME QUESTIONS FOR you: Are you a strong believer in God and Christ our Lord? Has your faith wavered at times? Is it wavering even now? Do you crave strengthening your belief in our Savior? Are you searching for him even now?

I have shared my Colorado experience on many occasions, giving my testimonial to different churches, my Kiwanis club, and several friends over lunch or dinner. One friend told me after our lunch, "Jim, I am jealous. I want that experience you had." Though I now feel blessed, I wouldn't want you or him to suffer the pain or stress I experienced that dreadful night last October!

I have a much less painful method for deepening your faith, which I strongly suggest. Please open your Bible to the book of Romans. Here the apostle Paul has written to his fellow believers in Rome, strengthening their faith and giving them hope for the future.

Below I excerpt selected verses from Romans 8, starting with verse 18 and continuing to the end of the chapter. My source is the NIV Student Bible; feel free to compare it with your own.

> I consider that our present sufferings are not worth comparing with the glory that will be reveled in us ... And we know that in all things God works for the good of those who love him, who have been called according to his purpose. ... What, then, shall we say in response to this? If God is for us, who can be against us? He who did not spare his own Son, but gave him up for us all- how will he not also, along with him, graciously give us all things? ... Who shall separate us from the love of Christ? Shall trouble or hardship or persecution or famine or nakedness or danger or sword? ... No, in all these things we are more than conquerors through him who loved us. For I am convinced that neither death nor life, neither angels nor demons, neither the present nor the future, nor any powers, neither height nor depth,

nor anything else in all creation, will be able to separate us from the love of God that is in Christ Jesus our Lord.

I wish you blessed happiness and contentment as you walk with our Lord.

—Jim Fogg

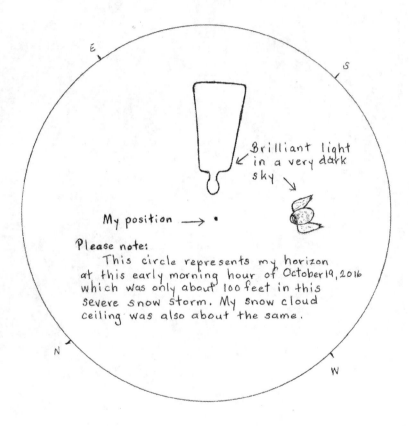

E

S

Brilliant light
in a very dark
sky

My position ———> •

Please note:
   This circle represents my horizon
at this early morning hour of October 19, 2016
which was only about 100 feet in this
severe snow storm. My snow cloud
ceiling was also about the same.

N

W

October 30, 2016

The Heavenly Vision

 **Revelation 1:9-20**
Common English Bible 500 NT

Central Question

What is my response to the risen Christ?

Scripture

Revelation 1:9-20

9 I, John, your brother who shares with you in the hardship, kingdom, and endurance that we have in Jesus, was on the island called Patmos because of the word of God and my witness about Jesus. 10 I was in a Spirit-inspired trance on the Lord's day, and I heard behind me a loud voice that sounded like a trumpet. 11 It said, "Write down on a scroll whatever you see, and send it to the seven churches: to Ephesus, Smyrna, Pergamum, Thyatira, Sardis, Philadelphia, and Laodicea." 12 I turned to see who was speaking to me, and when I turned, I saw seven oil lamps burning on top of seven gold stands. 13 In the middle of the lampstands I saw someone who looked like the Human One. He wore a robe that stretched down to his feet, and he had a gold sash around his chest. 14 His head and hair were white as white wool—like snow—and his eyes were like a fiery flame. 15 His feet were like fine brass that has been purified in a furnace, and his voice sounded like rushing water. 16 He held seven stars in his right hand, and from his mouth came a sharp, two-edged sword. His appearance was like the sun shining with all its power. 17 When I saw him, I fell at his feet like a dead man. But he put his right hand on me and said, "Don't be afraid. I'm the first and the last, 18 and the living one.

Jim Fogg

From: <staff@atlasnutritionwellnesscenter.com>
Date: Monday, November 27, 2017 3:16 PM
To: <foggy3@att.net>
Subject: Book Endorsement

An interesting life story from and American veteran that could have been tragic, yet turned out to be an incredible life changing event. A compelling read that puts life and eternity in perspective and speaks to the need for a strong will to survive for the sake of those you love. The book of Isaiah teaches us that the Holy Spirit, for believers, will direct your path;

Your own ears will hear him. Right behind you a voice will say, "This is the way you should go," whether to the right or to the left.
Isaiah 30:21

That voice was indeed tangible and ever present for Jim Fogg

I believe this real life experience will strengthen your faith and dependency in your walk with God.

Yours in Health,
Atlas Nutrition & Wellness Center
770-683-9202
Like us on ▓ Facebook
www.atlasnutritionwellnesscenter.com
www.AIChiro.com

Printed in the United States
By Bookmasters